Further Adventures in Monochrome

ALSO BY JOHN YAU

POETRY
Crossing Canal Street (1975)
The Reading of an Ever-Changing Tale (1977)
Sometimes (1979)
Broken Off by the Music (1981)
Corpse and Mirror (1983)
Radiant Silhouette: New & Selected Work 1974–1988 (1989)
Edificio Sayonara (1992)
Forbidden Entries (1996)
I Was a Poet in the House of Frankenstein (2000)
Borrowed Love Poems (2002)
Paradiso Diaspora (2006)
Exhibits (2010)

FICTION
The Sleepless Night of Eugene Delacroix (1980)
Hawaiian Cowboys (1995)
My Symptoms (1996)
My Heart Is That Eternal Rose Tattoo (2001)

COLLABORATIONS
Big City Primer (1991), with photographs by Bill Barrette
Berlin Diptychon (1995), with photographs by Bill Barrette
100 More Jokes from the Book of the Dead (2001), with Archie Rand
Ing Grish (2005), with Thomas Nozkowski

CRITICISM

In the Realm of Appearances: The Art of Andy Warhol (1993)

The United States of Jasper Johns (1996)

The Passionate Spectator: Essays on Art and Poetry (2006)

A Thing Among Things: The Art of Jasper Johns (2008)

EDITOR

Fairfield Porter: The Collected Poems with Selected Drawings (1985), with David Kermani

Fetish (1998)

Further Adventures in Monochrome

JOHN YAU

John Yau (signature)

COPPER CANYON PRESS

PORT TOWNSEND, WASHINGTON

Printed in the United States of America
Cover art: Katherine Bradford, *Super Flyer*

Copper Canyon Press is in residence at Fort Worden State Park in Port Townsend, Washington, under the auspices of Centrum. Centrum is a gathering place for artists and creative thinkers from around the world, students of all ages and backgrounds, and audiences seeking extraordinary cultural enrichment.

LIBRARY OF CONGRESS CATALOGING-IN-PUBLICATION DATA

Yau, John, 1950-
Further adventures in monochrome / John Yau.
    p. cm.
A collection of poems which have previously appeared in various journals, online magazines, and books.
ISBN 978-1-55659-396-3 (pbk. : alk. paper)
I. Title.

PS3575.A9F87 2012
811'.54—dc22

                                        2011050108
98765432 FIRST PRINTING

COPPER CANYON PRESS
Post Office Box 271
Port Townsend, Washington 98368

www.coppercanyonpress.org

Grateful acknowledgment is due the editors of the following journals, online magazines, and books, in which these poems first appeared:

American Poet, Big Bridge, Boulevard Magenta (Dublin), *Critical Quarterly, Denver Quarterly, Maggy, Narrative Magazine, Volt*

Genghis Chan: Private Eye I–VII appeared in *Radiant Silhouette: New and Selected Work 1974–1988* (Black Sparrow, 1989)

Genghis Chan: Private Eye VIII–XX appeared in *Edificio Sayonara* (Black Sparrow, 1992)

Genghis Chan: Private Eye XXI–XXVIII appeared in *Forbidden Entries* (Black Sparrow, 1996)

Genghis Chan: Private Eye XXIX–XXX appeared in *Borrowed Love Poems* (Penguin, 2002)

A Child's Vi[r]gil was published by Magnolia Editions as an Artist's Book (2010), illustrated by Norbert Prangenberg

One Hundred Poems was published by Magnolia Editions as an Artist's Book (2011), illustrated by Squeak Carnwath

The Missing Portrait was published by the Brodsky Center for Innovative Editions as an Artist's Book (2008), illustrated by Richard Tuttle

Exhibits was published as a chapbook by Letter Machine Editions (2010)

Black Square Editions published "Epithalamium" as a letterpress broadside

"Further Adventures in Monochrome" was the result of an invitation by Eric Lorberer, editor of *Rain Taxi,* and the Walker Art Center, Minneapolis, Minnesota to write a piece in response to the exhibition *Yves Klein: With the Void, Full Powers*. An earlier version, titled "Adventures in Monochrome," was presented at the Walker Art Center on November 11, 2010.

I would like to thank Hanna Andrews, Judy Brodsky, Gillian Conoley, Don and Era Farnsworth, Les Ferriss, Bonny Finberg, Adam Fitzgerald,

Noah Eli Gordon and Joshua Marie Wilkinson, Tom Jenks, Enrique Juncosa, Claudia La Rocco, Ben Lerner, John Martin, Ben Mirov, and Bin Ramke for providing homes for the poems.

For Eve and Cerise

PART ONE: Domestic Scenes and Studio Life

3   Chinese Nightingale

4   On Turning Sixty

5   A Child's Vi[r]gil

8   A Bungler Draped in Bangles Does Not a Burglar Make

13   Ill-Advised Love Poem

14   After Meng Hao-Jan

15   Ventriloquist

18   Day's Instruments

19   Father Knows Least

20   Epithalamium

22   Confessions of a Recycled Shopping Bag

PART TWO: Genghis Chan: Private Eye (1987–2011)

25   Genghis Chan: Private Eye I

26   Genghis Chan: Private Eye II

27   Genghis Chan: Private Eye III

28   Genghis Chan: Private Eye IV

29   Genghis Chan: Private Eye V

30   Genghis Chan: Private Eye VI

31   Genghis Chan: Private Eye VII

32   Genghis Chan: Private Eye VIII

33   Genghis Chan: Private Eye IX

34   Genghis Chan: Private Eye X

35   Genghis Chan: Private Eye XI

36   Genghis Chan: Private Eye XII

37   Genghis Chan: Private Eye XIII

38   Genghis Chan: Private Eye XIV

39   Genghis Chan: Private Eye XV

40   Genghis Chan: Private Eye XVI

41   Genghis Chan: Private Eye XVII

42   Genghis Chan: Private Eye XVIII (Rules of Conduct)

44   Genghis Chan: Private Eye XIX

45   Genghis Chan: Private Eye XX

46   Genghis Chan: Private Eye XXI

48   Genghis Chan: Private Eye XXII

50   Genghis Chan: Private Eye XXIII (Haiku Logbook)

56   Genghis Chan: Private Eye XXIV

57   Genghis Chan: Private Eye XXV

58   Genghis Chan: Private Eye XXVI

59   Genghis Chan: Private Eye XXVII

60   Genghis Chan: Private Eye XXVIII

61   Genghis Chan: Private Eye XXIX (Fourteen Ink Drawings)

62   Genghis Chan: Private Eye XXX

63   Genghis Chan: Private Eye XXXI
      (Hoboken Palace Gardens, After Renovations)

65   Genghis Chan: Private Eye XXXII

66   Genghis Chan: Private Eye XXXIII (First Ideogram)

67   Genghis Chan: Private Eye XXXIV (Second Ideogram)

68   Genghis Chan: Private Eye XXXV (Third Ideogram)

69   Genghis Chan: Private Eye XXXVI (Fourth Ideogram)

70   Genghis Chan: Private Eye XXXVII (Fifth Ideogram)

71   Genghis Chan: Private Eye XXXVIII (Sixth Ideogram)

72   Genghis Chan: Private Eye XXXIX (Seventh Ideogram)

73   Genghis Chan: Private Eye XL (Eighth Ideogram)

74   Genghis Chan: Private Eye XLI (Ninth Ideogram)

75   Genghis Chan: Private Eye XLII (Tenth Ideogram)

76   Genghis Chan: Private Eye XLIII

77   Genghis Chan : Private Eye XLIV

PART THREE: Revised Guide to the Ruins of a New City

81   Revised Guide to the Ruins of a New City (1)

82   Revised Guide to the Ruins of a New City (2)

83   Revised Guide to the Ruins of a New City (3)

84   One Hundred Poems

96   Exhibits

108   The Book of the Anonymous

PART FOUR: The Missing Portrait

115   The Missing Portrait (1)

117   The Missing Portrait (2)

119   The Missing Portrait (3)

121   The Missing Portrait (4)

122   The Missing Portrait (5)

PART FIVE: Further Adventures in Monochrome

Further Adventures in Monochrome

125   1) My fundamental self is at war with my multiple personalities

127   2) At present my paintings are invisible.

129   3) I recently

130   4) *I dwell in possibility,* Emily Dickinson

133   5) *Everything exists to end up in a book,* Stephane Mallarme

135   6) *For beauty is nothing but*

137   7) *Yves Klein Blue (Interlude)*

138   8) For me colors are living beings,

140   9) *The blue we bathe in is the blue we breathe....*

142   10) *(Robert Desnos and Yves Klein meet in the sky)*

143   11) *Trakl, Desnos, Klein*

144   12) *The blue of the sky, if we were to examine its many image values...*

145   13) An alchemist understands why I wrote: "My paintings are...

146   14) What I wanted from art was impossible.

147   15) Cubism was not the logical extension of Cézanne.

149   *About the Author*

PART ONE
Domestic Scenes and Studio Life

Chinese Nightingale

Hair burned white, teeth leaving one by one
More clouds dance past my crumbling hut
Pirouette and wave farewell. They will reach you
Long after I've turned to snow, your secrets still safe

More clouds dance past my crumbling hut
They opened a gas station at the wrong end of the telescope
Long after I turned to snow, your secrets still safe
Birds gathered along the wires, squirrels nodded in agreement

They opened a gas station at the wrong end of the telescope
I know because I sling hash in an empty noodle parlor
Birds gathered along the wires, squirrels nodded in agreement
In the watchtower guards snoozed and drooled on their armor

I know because I sling hash in an empty noodle parlor
Yesterday, she stopped wiping away her tears and smiled
In the watchtower guards snoozed and drooled on their armor
There are reasons for this, but no one can remember them

Yesterday, she stopped wiping away her tears and smiled
Hair turned white, teeth leaving one by one
There are reasons for this, but no one can remember them
Pirouette and wave farewell. They will reach you

On Turning Sixty

Hi, my name is Sir Geoffrey.
I am a limpid nerd.
This doesn't mean
I don't possess
many special qualities.
Or that I am not warm
even sensitive
when summoned
to the head of the line
as I just have been.
My skin tingles
when I pass a cage
full of rabbits.
I like chop suey
except when
it is crammed into a can.
I am a robust marshmallow
four days a week,
but I have been known
to ingest long
strings of meat
when they haven't been
individually wrapped
in plastic.
When you cross
the last threshold,
shed your sacred
dog mask, stranger,
and burst into
tears of unrepentant joy.
This is all I will ever ask.

A Child's Vi[r]gil

1.

Led by a talking
blue-and-red frog

a wooden cart
trundles treasure

up mosaic mountain
collection of talismans

in which heroes and heroines
have taken flight

skipped bail, jumped ship
left in the shadows

2.

Pink plastic figurine
missing arms

Two-headed turtle
pebbled green glass

Necklace of skulls—
each hides one

behind its
glass eyes

3.

For the moment
the remaining idols

remain idle
in this idyll

set among stones

4.

Starting to slender into fluid
Fitted out with wings
Could not cease peeking
Near stands a deep pool
Not even more songs flowing crookedly could halt the clouds
Hidden antlers, beating of wings
Keeps and preserves the moist
Smitten, seized, hasty
More rain from her tunic
You cannot become against the taken
Pokes her stretching out
Reduced to a disagreeable substance
After these, and trickling
Once more dimmed the stars

5.

Stretches garment
over her cries

so that harm
might be kept

from becoming
an official decree

Worn down
by lavish gifts

A grumble rose
about her

6.

Do tell of the trophy
installed in Olympus
that caused feathers to appear

Their concealment
delighted the clouds
Would bed down in the distance

The next was clattering
in a horse
pitched over beneath its warm glistening

Was last to prove
Spare, bent, sped on
Hair laid out in a row

In the tall grass
something small
and shiny is found

A Bungler Draped in Bangles Does Not a Burglar Make

Don't ask me to tell you
what I look like now.
I haven't the foggiest idea
what has happened to me.
Getting up on stage,
cupping a microphone,
facing an expectorating audience
scares the sap out of this tree.
Let me start over
without pausing
at the artificial pond
surrounded by
poisonous vines.
Concocting parents
born in different,
distant countries
has advantages,
though I can't be
too explicit about them
at this stage
in human evolution.
According to anonymous sources,
the fact that they met
on a rainy night in Rangoon
might strike indiscriminate
readers as a miracle.
It was the chubby hands
covering the genitalia
that seemed out of place.
My grandfather died
when I was six.
I have hated
the smell of laundry

detergent ever since.
Haven't you ever been in a situation
where you love someone special,
but you are not sure
that they are special enough?
At first, the yellow strips
blended well with my face.
The following frames
are to be viewed
in rapid succession,
while resting in
an armchair of suitable girth
and durability
under pressure.
Evil pandas
roam the earth,
disguised as waiters
with big hands and spotted shirts.
Later, I spent much of my childhood
in a model train store
waiting for the black chimney
to stop at the platform
across from where my parents
minded their own business.
Lingering of this sort is bad behavior
when it occurs in a shopping mall
named after a former mayor.
We emerged from the evil-
smelling taxi and found
that the autumnal weather
was no longer there to greet us.
I realized that I was going to
have to stop being a troublesome troll
if I wanted to make further strides
in my quest for nobility.

I married an aeronautics engineer.
I didn't realize that I liked
the telephone company
far more than is considered
healthy by industry standards.
Soon after I stopped
wearing straps.
The other night I stood
alone in my neighbor's shower,
contemplating shaving
my shriveled armpits
when I was compelled to consider
what weakness
in my character
caused me to turn out as I did.
The link you followed
may be expired
or put out with the trash
that never made it back
from the magazine store.
Among the several things
working against me
is a spigot of intelligence,
which is constantly
being blocked by outside forces.
The fact that my father
was a celebrated charlatan
has little bearing
on what I am about to tell you.
There is something comical
about being Chinese
in a time of overcrowding
and downsizing.
The soap I use
smells so good

I tried to eat it.
I am very excited
to be teaching
another cooking class
based on mutual frugality.
I build xylophones
out of bamboo and bubble gum,
and sell them to blind musicians.
You need to be close
to the parking lot of a midsized hospital
if you are thinking about
going out in weather like this.
I'm pretty sure I won't have to tell any of you
just how unsanitary hotel rooms are.
Being detached from your corporate status
can cause panic among the uninitiated.
I wear striped pajamas in winter,
when dark skies unroll
their carpets of nails across the lake.
I have a sampler in my brain
that takes what is said and feeds it to me
with an electronic spoon.
I am not a pollution-belching monstrosity.
Once you've experienced
how profitable and *simple* it is
to develop your own digital identity,
you'll probably forget
that you ever existed as anything else.
My hind leg raised
I am an ant peeing in your syrup.
Having failed to light my nose on fire
when I turned twenty-three,
I prided myself on being
one of the walking wounded.
My motto is "fast, cheap, and wood."

I learned that you can only go so far,
and then you can't stop thinking about it.
I caught a case of postnasal depression,
the world never smelled the same again.
My worries began to recede
once I donned the mask of the Dead Sea mouse.
I know that I will never find the real me
because I spend all my time submitting
erotic stories to the new editor.
We didn't end up in bed or a straightjacket,
which is why I am writing to tell you
to start planning your birthday party.
On Sundays, I like to eat steak tartare,
watch vampire movie reruns with my dog.
In the meantime, I promise
to stop being a butterfly
long enough to learn
the names of endangered flowers.

Ill-Advised Love Poem

Come live with me
And we will sit

Upon the rocks
By shallow rivers

Come live with me
And we will plant acorns

In each other's mouth
It would be our way

Of greeting the earth
Before it shoves us

Back into the snow
Our interior cavities

Brimming with
Disagreeable substances

Come live with me
Before winter stops

To use the only pillow
The sky ever sleeps on

Our interior cavities
Brimming with snow

Come live with me
Before spring

Swallows the air
And birds sing

After Meng Hao-Jan

Every Friday I carry home a small bird

Upon which I lavish all my attention

Neither green nor red hilltops lure me

I do not speculate about ceaseless wonders

Those passing overhead can see

In winter I drink tea by the window

Stars shine through my reflection

Occasionally I go out and see if I might

Find another remote and insubstantial form

Ventriloquist

For Jasper Johns

One night I dreamed that I got up the next morning
I went out, bought materials, and began to paint
The next night I dreamed that I got up and began

That's the way it was done
Those days have stayed there
Sometimes I sometimes don't

I would be responsible to it in the present tense
I was in the winter once and I decided I liked going out
I decided I would be it in the winter

The lightbulb involved two stones and a miscalculation
I got up the next morning and dreamed that I went out
Winter was done and I hesitated to take any

I would not say that
I would not say that
Written upside down and backward

I think this part of a thing close to a model
I am interested in which suggests the world
Leaves more air around the elements

I rarely travel
I travel a great deal between here
And when I have to

There is a drawing that shows the end of the world
And there is this little figure standing there
I got a job and looked at these things in books

I made three from a child's arm
I thought it would become large
I thought it would be easier to use than avoid

I dreamed that I went out a great deal
I got up and began to be responsible
I decided I would be involved in a miscalculation

I am interested in what is, and what is not
I try to find a way to leap from one to another
I don't like any, least of all mine

You have to leave that as itself
And begin begin again
I imagine everything has its role

I don't know what I would like them to do
It's hard to reconstruct without lying
There seemed to be a kind of catching fire

That any be anywhere and anything
That anywhere be anything and any
That anything be any and anywhere

What distinguishes one from the other
The mirror is not in the mirror
The dots can be gathered into a line of stewed tomatoes

An imagined unit the square of
The height of enclosed by
Will include difficulty of determining

I made materials that I dreamed up
I went out and began winter and decided
I don't understand what can be implied

I am neither hopeful nor not hopeful
I think of them as cartoons
I formed some cheap idea

I have always been terrified of walking into a room
And telling people what to do
It could have many effects, but one wants to get rid of the category

Every period is a period of unsettled language
I've never been able to because I couldn't speak
I read this and the name stuck in my head

Day's Instruments

They say we should write about our misery-
soaked selves, parade our inadequacies
before all, pad about in cracked slippers
Why speak about other things when you cannot mean
what you say, when meaning retreats before every attempt
to give it a face, make it something to look at, as it stares
back, gripping our tattered coils, a green ocean
calmly embracing our bubbles rising toward air.
They say we should write without expectation,
in rooms where walls are deaf to invocations and imbroglios,
that we should implode with delight at every silence
that greets us. How little they have learned from our refusals.

2.

We took the words we were given, severed earthworms
jumping and twisting in our hands, clouds of red dust
extruding from their skin, yes, we took these words,
gulped them down, knowing they were not ours,
and used them. This way and that way,
we used the words we were given,
words we were told no longer held meaning,
their surfaces porous, their sides cracked open,
and we poured what we could from them,
over our heads set on fire, our feet
sticking up from the earth.

Father Knows Least

Father liked to say that things were different back then, that even the
snowflakes were larger, more fulfilling, especially if you were afflicted
with a hunger that only snowflakes could cure, but mother disagreed,
standing her ground, fierce and toothsome—a tall glass of dish soap
weathering a storm of filthy laundry. This duet of bits and pieces first
gained notice as the Third Neo-Mexican Symphony, a name that
hardly does the event justice.

Once they began soaring over the dining room table set for six, with
the next-door neighbors, the Doggs, a ragged bunch of drop-in guests,
sucking on martinis and thumbs, there was no telling what might
happen when father grabbed the gleaming blade over the mantelpiece,
where (he liked to say) sharp objects belong, yelling "the broad battle-
axe deserves a good sacking," but since we were children who had
not attained our full height, the growth spurt parceled out by our
parsimonious parson, we closed our eyes, and began living in another
city on a plain of smokestacks, and, on weekends, visiting a faraway farm

where

mother and father are playing whist, while we wag our tails and cavort
with the mice that patiently constructed the Margarine Line dividing
China from France. When you do this, you also have an opportunity
to do that with less. This is the case of the crust being thicker than
the interior, cans of peaches bought in a department store known for
its salesmen, who had the peculiar habit of helping dowagers fit their
thickly encrusted feet into rows of smooth shoes made from animals
that lurk in corners. After many hours of practice, we learned to slurp
the yellow nectar gathering on the ends of our chins. Wound licking
became a national pastime we could not do without. Even now, after
all the years of economic surplus handed up to those more fortunate
than us.

Epithalamium

For Benjamin La Rocco and
Linnea Paskow on May 30, 2011

Now oceanic span
in ikon silo
pose koan praise

Oilcan airman joins woman limner in romance aisle

(I will)

O Enamor Owl
O manila animal
O enamel llama
Our paws poke limber oracle

Lions unseal carmine wines
Lemon sake
Roman ales

Plink plonk polka bolero
Canal skoal opens melon arbor
Pink piano spins miracle romance
Nacre piano spins banjo clamor
Maroon ocarina boreal paean
Awaken lips on noble jerboa
Arcane merlin inner ninja
Join raccoon lapis on acorn isle
Pines croon in bloom combo
Inks link winks on camera
Amenable nameable linen amble
Enable balm élan jam
Walk swap plan lips speak

Anima Brain Cornea
Spoken plain
BE A POEM

Confessions of a Recycled Shopping Bag

I used to be a plastic bottle

I used to be scads of masticated wattle

I used to be epic spittle, aka septic piddle

I used to be a pleasant colleague

I used to be a radiant ingredient

I used to be a purple polyethylene pony

I used to be a phony upload project

I used to be a stony blue inhalant

I used to be a family-size turquoise bottle

I used to be a domesticated pink bubble

I used to be a pleasant red colleague

I used to be a beaming cobalt emollient

I used to be a convenient chartreuse antidepressant

Genghis Chan: Private Eye I

I was floating through a cross section
with my dusty wineglass, when she entered,
a shivering bundle of shredded starlight.
You don't need words to tell a story,
a gesture will do. These days,
we're all parasites looking for a body
to cling to. I'm nothing more
than riffraff splendor drifting past the runway.
I always keep a supply of lamprey lipstick around,
just in case.
                          She laughed,
A slashed melody of small shrugs.
It had been raining in her left eye.
She began: a cloud or story
broken in two maybe four places,
wooden eyelids, and a scarf of human hair.
She paused: I offer you dervish bleakness
and glistening sediment.
                                        It was late
and we were getting jammed in deep.
I was on the other side, staring at
the snow-covered moon pasted above the park.
A foul lump started making promises in my voice.

Genghis Chan: Private Eye II

I looked down,
more slender
than I expected

          She was
wearing white under white
gray blond curls dropped back
turned into a block

Across the room, a mirror
had been drained from the top

Clouds buzzed above burgeoning trees
their neat brochures

Their apartment had been flung open
ceiling nibbled at the corners

They had lasted longer than we calculated
refusing to hang up the other's ashes

An ignorant sponge, I had been summoned
to the gate of no mistakes

In less than half a pedal of time
I would be entering the hyena zone

Genghis Chan: Private Eye III

We surfed out of the alley,
the stories our parents told us
trailing behind, like angry yellow toads

You spoke first:
One of my ancestral coupons
composed the bulldozer anthem
Perhaps she too was waiting
for the bumper-crop showers
to subside, another dust mote picker
in a long line of lovelorn imports
Yes, I too was stymied by the animal of music
and the shadow its breath sent through history

I wanted to tell you
about the bank teller and the giant,
the red moths hovering above their heads

I wanted to tell you
about the gizmo pit and kinds of sludge
I have cataloged during my investigation

I wanted to tell you
about how the sun
dissolved all of this long ago

leaving us in different rooms

registered under different names

Genghis Chan: Private Eye IV

Rusted Pundit, Throttled Chin

I was turned by a tendril adrift,
pale freckled skin bathed
in insect iridescence,
lips sucked through a straw

Tonight's sampler stops
beside the dialed states,
showroom padlocks coiled
around the vantage points,
gasps clogged in the spray

She was a farm of concrete
cleanly poured, and I
—the quarantined flash—
was tilting above Newt Falls,
its glossy stanzas of imitation snow

Hours of sigh practice loomed ahead

Genghis Chan: Private Eye V

You looked and said:
I spiraled above a forest of necktie splendor
A wooden trembler
Hovering above the jet lag lanes
A lost shrieker, I hesitated

You looked up and said:
A glass frog with green bones and one red vein
The streets are lizards in profile
We have strayed from the beehive slag

You looked up and said:
Written rewritten blue dust
Falls through my dried tongue

Genghis Chan: Private Eye VI

I am just another particle cloud gliding across the screen

A swamp chanter doodling on the margins of the abyss

I prefer rat backs to diplomatic curls

I am the owner of one pockmarked tongue

I park it on the hedge between sure bets and bad business

Genghis Chan: Private Eye VII

You will remember the tourist's jawbone
And the end of the erotic age

You will remember how to number
The customized stones of Spartan psychoanalysis

You will be nice to yourself and regret it
You will undress in front of a window overlooking a prison

You will speak to the driver of a blue hearse
You will grasp someone's tongue with your teeth and pull

You will prefer the one that bleeds on the carpet
To the one that drools on your sleeve

Genghis Chan: Private Eye VIII

I plugged in the new image fertilizer
And complained to my inaudible copy

We did tour the best spots
Trying to attract basic signs of pity

Touched a disaster every now and then
And remained ridiculous and understaffed

Now I am clamped to the desk
Unraveling thought's stunted projectiles

Had I been a chameleon
I would have crossed my eyes

So as to look more like you
Than your silver reflection

I would have hummed to the statue
Inside your black eyes and black tongue

I would have memorized its tongue

Genghis Chan: Private Eye IX

I was headed toward a surprise I could not return,
Its twisted little forehead and clinging grin
Waiting beside the fountain of cakes

Who dropped the water-bearing rocks
Through the mail slots? Why does the moon
Admire the rich, their diamond curls

Glassine beneath bags of yellow dust?
Why does the sun carry its entrails around?
I was babbling before I started,

My mouth glued to the lips
Floating above the monkey clouds.
Foam spilled from its huddle of frozen intentions,

Each drop armed with an emblem.
Lucky, no gun is glistening
Beside the puddles I drift down Happy Avenue

Genghis Chan: Private Eye X

Wine-steeped clouds
Ignite city's rim

Bubbles float to
Roof of mouth

Burst into clods
Spooning wooden crumbs

From reptile reruns
I ride notes down

Stick scratching
Dirt walls

Axis blurt
Scrawny rabble

Watch indelible water
Seep through clocks

Genghis Chan: Private Eye XI

Small hunks drift
Rumble across their shoes

Porous metal scrapes
Top rung of hired dreamers

Surrounded by clumped tongues
Fenced-out eyes

Insistent paddle drifter
Smeller of candies

I patrol the mattress-stained windows
Twiddle down hours

A service examiner of bodies
Pumped into the fast lanes of alley grass

I keep my heads in my lap
Train small turtles to cry

I am a piece of cake
Stacked against the company wall

Genghis Chan: Private Eye XII

The apology corpses watch
Little matchsticks of wit

Illuminate the park
Slender stalks are goosed

From their tripods
Mounted on

Chubby dinner plates
I am outside of

The helium conference
Hopping from grunt to grunt

A battered jabberer
Launches his coffee

Streams out his arms
Whispers

I received my certificate
To practice being humus

I too am a yellow lamp
Bolted to the elephant sky

Genghis Chan: Private Eye XIII

It is hard to keep pretending
You are a yellow chink
In a hall of dusty linen

You begin believing
You are just another handkerchief
Wiping away the laundress's tears

Genghis Chan: Private Eye XIV

My new yellow name
Was ladled over

Your installment plan
Another blue dollar special

Bubbling below
The Avenue of Ovens

Used star slots
Their three laces

A bomb in a raincoat
Was inserted later

Shell or shill
Black pills to slip

The old horse down
I was fired on slanted legs

Copying your words
Onto matches and axes

As if they were gods
With wooden bellies

Genghis Chan: Private Eye XV

You broke the star
I pinned to the ceiling

that stacked sky
I swam beneath

toward the window
where you were landing

watching a yellow moonlit
race of bold potatoes

outrunning the new elite
the stain clingers and honey babble

You were a music taker
at home in the spit

Genghis Chan: Private Eye XVI

Another mule in the spoon trade

Among pigeon rankers
of the slowest crank

I danced among
fossil bunglers
gelatinous geezers

A crutch program
gone soft in the lead
slithering up the pegs

I imitated others
leading to the ladder of sighs

Genghis Chan: Private Eye XVII

I was the wood doctor
who made mouse calls

pluck for more
I stuffed bullet boxes

with yellow jelly snacks
counted raked lumps

from the neck of my bruise
I was a name staller

heisting scalped hearts
a golden waged

hardware jolter
in blue stuffers

wallowing daintily
in the mutt routine

Genghis Chan: Private Eye XVIII
(Rules of Conduct)

Follow the pimple instructions
You are supposed to

Splash them down
Scream side first

Spot a diamond
Mooch peddler

Stalking his puddle
To the corner number

His wrist of occupations
Swindling the best drams

From her flaccid rustle
Steam out a defective colonel

Selecting moles to hoist
Beside a fellow sled buoy

Store the verbs
Of a rock making

Mock raker
Stilled by

The smiles of easy soot
Sifting his pay

Grease the tines
Of every genuine article

Transmitting
Radio wives

Through granular flight
Spill the inventory of stars

We sold to the voices
Stained above our beds

Genghis Chan: Private Eye XIX

My stamped mother
used to fling to me

All stones lead to home
Go easy on the turtle pie

gored down
at doom temperature

Cast a cold
and dirty style

on every yellow
leaf of lassitude

glistening beneath
the grappled fly

My stamped mother
used to fling me

and I
her lump of muck

would fling back
all the riveted stones

I could dandle
on my wasted plea

the chink of meat
we knew that linked us

to the junk
going by

Genghis Chan: Private Eye XX

I posed
as a cookie
fortune smeller

I sold
the stale delays
your parents pranced to

the old bunch
gathered beside
the evening stalk

I squeezed
the liars alive

I bent their bubbles
around air's broken coat

Genghis Chan: Private Eye XXI

I am a hat softener
In the trade confession

A belly-down carpet stamp
Jerks are my toys

I spray them
With my battering ham

Over-easy side order
Flies to grow

Slime covers us tall
Flags flow meaner

On the other tide
Puddle around with stack beans

Slab the spotted pig
Before he drivels

This grind of activity
Flavors the rest

First muskets and mouse caps
Then caskets and caboose taps

Lotion drains down
Your past leaves

Burns the flock
Back to one

These are the rodents
You oil in your tree

The heads you snip off
At the wreck

When gum plays to spoon
Tide of the mouth

You have to screech
Around your powdered elf

Tune your acne clumps
To the smallest dimes

Genghis Chan: Private Eye XXII

Aquarium night steers
two intersected occupants

(a motel I and the one
inside its vowel remnant)

toward a library of ledges
Stack doodle know-how

And lake metal shivers
A frigid stare card

I (or my tongue)
am the lizard

who bakes
your last animal residue

A tropical fossil haze
in an empty

farmhouse suit
Potion cogs

distributed beneath
the neural

carport
A limousine

transmission
aerialist

sparkling
stewed spew

on the pyramid floor
I or the one

curled around
my voice

celebrate the humid glow
of another radius

burning the staircase of
its insect logic

Genghis Chan: Private Eye XXIII
(Haiku Logbook)

1.

Feed him his lights
Poke down wallet sniffer
Probe hoisted tar dispute

2.

Silk crave
Worn buckles slipped tight
Crawl on tide rock

3.

Linger and blunder
Slave dunks cooking for pearls
Failed to let dust control his fur spree

4.

School pigeon hot in rack
Circus hat moth fear
Leaf gnasher in girdle triumph

5.

Toasted of his wooden thighs
Flight ladles yearning their slicks
Empty star on a valley sheet

6.

Could feel the flute in his glands
Young wild sputtering into his cursed zone
Savage hex in retail lobby

7.

Investigate domestic squirrel
Donkey liner puddling his horse
Horizontal rain delay

8.

Idaho rooster fed in wooden slipper
Slack addict combing in hunk yard
Bend fools around calloused dumb

9.

Spilled his ruts over sawdust shore
Slow knots disturb gym lass
Lunch his flights out

10.

Flies never lie
Sediment selection trail
Ride behind trick stall

11.

Snow looter in a feathered gab
Nuzzling pansy growler
Loot to spill

12.

Scalding dump steer
Oiling the wool
Slump diner over boulder

13.

Burden of fruit calls upon you
Stumps from an abandoned reject
Spud dude in rotten candy stains

14.

Corner blasted door owner
Rents out of cape
Lust burns to act residential

15.

Tells child for seeded monkey
Curtain praiser
In the wine of fire

16.

Stare of lookers grabbed by strife
Face-high flood rakes mall
Shark storage crank

17.

Cloud agency floats belly cup
Dish crosser unlegged by can
Thigh lotion signals makeup fall

18.

Lust whim for rope
Born to bruise
Pixie crate

19.

Leather glass border
Fed on treat rustler
Scalawag sound unit

20.

Grime scavenger
Branch of cotton posed skids
Spore another wit

21.

Bound in rusty hotel broom
Turn the key and kit brighter
Whittled sighs almost paved him

22.

Potion score drifts through pails
Little piles of dirty honey
Slick to climb over incoming raves

23.

Plum ox bashed lead
Wig coiler thrashed to sound
Cost soggy toy scout route

24.

Traffic cram in funnel
Tithe trace in milk bandage
Muscle can stoves the hunch

25.

Two-cheek bonus spray
Ground runaway style
Bout of order

26.

Retain bunny robot impresario
Lease placate room
Exhibition kiss

27.

Revisits drapery in a winch
Scrambled the sea quencher
Short groom drama flays the spare

28.

Plover and gout
Unretainable lotion quickness
Vile under

29.

Bank clobber miss lap
Spotted race crack lasher
Earned his graft

30.

Returned gift plodder
Tall signs
Point to sudden breath

Genghis Chan: Private Eye XXIV

Grab some
Grub some

Sub gum
Machine stun

Treat pork
Pig feet

On floor
All fours

Train cow
Chow lane

Dice played
Trade spice

Makes fist
First steps

Genghis Chan: Private Eye XXV

Dimple sample
Rump stump

Dump fun
Dim sum

Slum rubble
Gong sob

Strong song
Oolong

Rinky-dink
Trinket rock

Duck walk
Talk muck

Genghis Chan: Private Eye XXVI

Honking
Hong Kong

Road map
Toad face

Hong king
"Store lord"

Dead cold
Unload

Old gold
Smoke gripe

Fan stamp
Dance step

Stamp fan
Sampan

Gunk junk
Lug wretch

Wrench nut
Cut stench

Genghis Chan: Private Eye XXVII

Moo goo
Milk mush

Guy pan
Piss pot

Genghis Chan: Private Eye XXVIII

Droll moll
Cool doll

Key chain
Chin key

Sly jive
Yell high

Genghis Chan: Private Eye XXIX
(Fourteen Ink Drawings)

Mirror   film   stain
Gown   tiger   glass
Canopy   powder   bell
Mulberry   blister   festival
Boat   portrait   box
Vermillion   chestnut   cloud
Milk   shadow   moon
Breeze   identical   face
Ink   ladder   jar
Orchid   chimney   tongue
Parachute   sword   wave
Groom   motel   coffee
Anvil   clock   hair
Condom   audience   dog

Genghis Chan: Private Eye XXX

Shoo war
Torn talk

Ping towel
Pong toy

Salted sap
Yellow credit

Hubba doggo
Bubba patootie

Wig maw
Mustard tongue

Genghis Chan: Private Eye XXXI
(Hoboken Palace Gardens, After Renovations)

We sat beneath a webbed and vaulted sky
Crammed with mechanical mockingbirds

Trying to live up to their name
A green-and-white cab came and waited

Until the last bullet was swept up
Stuffed in a transparent envelope

The old driver puffed on a red cigar
Which he said he found in the library

Two nurses wrapped me in a pink blanket
The fat one handed my sister a plastic bone

After the bricks unraveled, and the tornado
Collapsed on the outskirts of town

Like an old man whose anger
Has finally stabbed him

The story gets progressively colder
An uncle stood up and peed in his coffee cup

Wanda got a job with the rodeo as an assistant cook
Purple Bill finally learned the real reason

Why his neighbors called him "Esmerelda Desdemona"
When he started his fancy jalopy

I could have told you
Another white lie

I could have heaped it
On the mountain

Gathering before you
Perhaps it would have

Even been the truth
The whole truth

But I wouldn't have known it,
Not then and not now

When the air gets thick and stuffy like this
My brain turns into a dog dish

I circle
My tongue hanging out like a wet flannel sleeve

I wore your underwear to work the other day
But it did not make me feel as sexy as I thought it would

Why have you stopped tapping your foot
I was just beginning to get in the mood

To swing down from my branch and sing
That sweet smell is the soup starting to rot

I remain, as always, your disobedient servant

Genghis Chan: Private Eye XXXII

Dear Gerrymander
Personality Devotee

Dear Voice
Register of Iniquity

Dear Chloroform
Dear Pyramid

Dear Poetry Corpse
Wrapped in Key of Seed

Dear Chrysanthemum
Bud in Black Pajamas

Dear Angel Cake
Wrist Banger

Dear Burn Down the House
Run Amok

Dear Scantily Clad
Weekly Update

Dear Pagoda Red
Singapore Sling

Orient Blush
Your names are

Plastic raindrops
Gathering on

Blue ceiling
Above burning sky

Genghis Chan: Private Eye XXXIII
(First Ideogram)

BEE WEAR

FLEE ADVICE

FOREST STRANGER

Genghis Chan: Private Eye XXXIV
(Second Ideogram)

SHIT UP

F   U

GUT

SUM   CENTS

Genghis Chan: Private Eye XXXV
(Third Ideogram)

SACK of RICE

———————————

SACK HER VICE

———————————

SACK • RIFF • ICE

Genghis Chan: Private Eye XXXVI
(Fourth Ideogram)

SAY CRUD
SANK DUMB

MORE

TRUE
BULL

A
HEAD

Genghis Chan: Private Eye XXXVII
(Fifth Ideogram)

FUR REIGN   HACK SENSE

———————————————————

Ewe Ear

Damn

Every Wear

Genghis Chan: Private Eye XXXVIII
(Sixth Ideogram)

NEW BODY

LEAVES HEAR

A LIE

Genghis Chan: Private Eye XXXIX
(Seventh Ideogram)

D   I   S   G   U   I   S   E
_____

the limit

Genghis Chan: Private Eye XL
(Eighth Ideogram)

BEE

LEAVE IT

A LOAN

Genghis Chan: Private Eye XLI
(Ninth Ideogram)

SUM WEAR

MORE

THAN THEY KNOW

Genghis Chan: Private Eye XLII
(Tenth Ideogram)

D E W

the bright things

Genghis Chan: Private Eye XLIII

Long hours toiling at the terminal

Beady eyes stuck in a cantaloupe

Exotic wildlife in easily disposable jars

All yours for only a fraction of a lifetime

I was found in a field of leaves and overturned squirrels

A great disappointment awaits you until further notice

Join together and cry for your temporary place in line

Mortification is the least of my inflictions

Refresh the parts of yourself that remain enamored of the dark

Igor, Iago, and Ichabod sniff the love seat before reaching a consensus

And all along you thought I was a zombie making naughty noises at you

Genghis Chan: Private Eye XLIV

Summer's predictable ascent

Tenants barking at night

Heckles and hackles

I watch last drops of obedience

Flee the little mortals

Gnawing filth in schoolyard

Stop moping at the dinner table

Come on and go outside

Everywhere you look the sky ends in dust

PART THREE

Revised Guide to the Ruins of a New City

Revised Guide to the Ruins of a New City (1)

Children gather on the ledges of a flattened world
Laugh at lightbulbs punctuating sky
Exploding stars armory full of broken arms
The city as storage facility beneath scattered clouds
City of bone fragments stadiums lined with human dust
Tear-streaked windows overlooking subterranean civilizations
Tea-stained widows in drowned parking garages lined with lighted candles
City tethered to the Museum of Gravity and its bottles of copyrighted smoke
Eclipsed failures
Dead letter department tunnel to escape jubilation's iron grip
Necropolis post office billboards hearken hawks convulsing above swollen river
In celestial panopticon postcard delivered to dead bettors office
By one of the working dead
Their swank blather
Two girls digging for hazardous materials
Such as underwear and lipstick
Black nylon bandages
In a storage facility
Full of streetcars swans anemic residue
Ink dripping into porcelain bowls
Street of astral rejects
Neither native nor nonnative
Syrupy sky
Like clock hands that never meet
No luck is the best luck of all
City as theme park where visitors
Visit themselves in another life
Theme park as city of fragments
Constant stream of headless horses
Waiting for televisions to begin their morning vigil

Revised Guide to the Ruins of a New City (2)

Deluded, denuded, diluted
Sanctuary
Between sky's brackets and bracelets
Courtroom of stars
Beneath moth-fluttering eyelids
Under inclination of vertical to walk upright amidst
A guest a guess aghast a ghost of
There will be no more filings in this cabinet of curiosities
Trash receptacle of human taste
Sullen sponges irritated grid
Necessary and unnecessary equivocations
Central climate control breached by worms
Scorned ganglia
In this incomplete cartoon of damaged data and exit samples
Swell in the slime of sex
Protozoan galas stricken with hula hoopla
Story injected with sap from sapient slivers
Writing withering on its branches of frippery
How does this sky create itself in our eyes
Pink and poisonous as tongue
Swelling in mouth of dead love
Who feeds the palimpsest
That reads itself
Into clouded ceiling and sky
Snow the only perfume left of our dwindling supplies

Revised Guide to the Ruins of a New City (3)

Gut baffling
Here is the proper opprobrium
To stick in latest mouth to garnish news
Delirium before the calm
Torso capture renders fat into rain
Slaughtered torrents
Relentless sanguinity pushes back darkening scarlet sky
Filling recently added diploma clouds
Coming concentric flicker as night advances its pawns
Swollen claw moon cleans its engine
More smoke circulates ventilated barrages
Alone in sum of summer's tent
Trade plunder gushes degraded spurts
Decimation without hindsight of client pool
Desperado busts, incandescent hall, obelisk shadow, fluted letters
More mirrors needed for shining populace
When everybody is everybody else
Flammable fleece glitter
In amnesia shop necessitates full gamut array
Slop inside electrical plug decaying chandelier sky
Swallowed in elaborate sentences
Refusing to escape their lips in public
Internal combustion moon above hospital's blazing rooftops
Crowns ephemeral anatomy
Advice repetition service in ink of remedial messages
Back door nearly sky
Flooding whirlpool wishes
Strike out for heaven humming trophy

One Hundred Poems

Mercury

The Messenger is also known as Hydra, the many-headed monster with a poisonous dog's body; and each head multiplies every time someone lops it off.

Labyrinth

I can't remember why I was put here in the first place.

Universal

There is something in it for everyone.

First Prose Poem

In 1456, Bartolomeo Fazio described Jan van Eyck's *mappa mundi* as the most perfect work of its time, and that its bird's-eye view was from a higher vantage point than any bird could fly.

Biography of Li Po and Tu Fu

They were intoxicated with everything but themselves.

What Became of Me?

A piece of smelly meat limping up and down stairs.

Warning Sign

Please do not remove any more dust from the moon.

All Eyes Were on X

There is no known cure for this.

What Did We Learn?

A few things that helped some of us stay here a little longer.

Numerology

True love meets its perfect partner.

Fortune

You have got to be kidding me.

Mr. Flummox Addresses the Assembly

I have a good mind, but I won't waste it on you.

Dear Jetsam and Flotsam, Snoozy and Woozy

Greetings from the Terminal of Wounded Shepherds

Note on the Proper Preparation of "Supreme Surprise"

Until recently, there was no known substitute for "elephant drool."

The Most Important Rule Regarding Rodent Regalia

There should be nothing that is gray or brown, and this includes epaulets, buttons, and tassels.

Slow Dance

Either the "Brooklyn Eyelid Sag" or "Death Becomes You."

Tall Red Urn in the Shape of a Skyscraper

Voted most efficient storage unit for the moon's ashes.

Curious

What makes you want to wag your tail?

The Glass Eye on the Mantelpiece

The family gathers at noon, and waits for it to blink once more.

Exhortation

Please use our toilet paper the next time you visit.

Writing Machine

Made of silver threads and leather, this artificial hand once belonged to a poet.

Time Flies

When you remember to bring your wings to the swap meet.

I Can't Tell You How Happy I Am to Be Here

In accordance with the author's wishes, this space has been left blank.

Fairy Tale

Just married, a bride and groom enter a dark forest, never to be seen or heard from again.

Fairy Tale (2)

A horse whistles sharply, and its master comes running, carrying a silver tray.

Tropical Postcard

A black-and-white kitten climbs through a fence with a lizard's tail dangling from its mouth.

Familiar Complaint

My egg rolls look like dirty tube socks.

Arrangement and Rearrangement

Love, Jetsam and Woozy, Flotsam and Snoozy

Zeus and Juno

A species that is able to successfully disguise itself.

Client

A person becomes convinced that you possess an arcane body of knowledge.

Scarecrows, Hedgerows, and Hedgehogs

Sleep will punish those you fail to rescue.

Store Motto

No more muss or fuss
When you bring us
Your broken blunderbuss

Paradiso Diaspora

Silent inlets

Credit

If you must know, the cars rusting in the yard are amulets.

The Eighth Dwarf

Doozy (aka Woozy) was last seen heading south on Interstate 74.

Sign

No matter what else you do, please remember to wash your hands before leaving tonight's performance.

Act Three

The light didn't go out at the last moment, you did.

Advertisement

Office desk kept in cloud suitcase.

A Pack of Barking Dogs

The image of you that you know best is waiting for another touch-up.

Blood Bank

"I am a magnet for mosquitoes."

Crime Scene

Dough nut, donut, do not, dew knot.

Indispensable

We have made available all kinds of products for people of small accomplishment.

Sage

Sometimes a wise man, other times a shrub with purple and white flowers, used in cooking.

Disaster

The tip of the iceberg is missing.

Complaint

I can't complain.

Danger, the Hotel Swimming Pool

is full of all kinds of belly-fish.

Dessert Precedes Disease

Spotted dick.

Dogs Do

dog doo.

Sex Doll/Doll Sex

I am a full-service cervix waiting to service you.

Familiar Undiscovered Territory

There isn't anything else like it.

Anonymous and Particular

What we are in the face of time.

Newest Anagram Spy Camera

Snoop Spoon

Crime Scene

Is this *is* his or not?

What Didn't We Learn?

A few things that can help some of us stay here a little longer.

Variation on Earlier Poem

I spotted Dick carrying a plate of spotted dick.

Bruised Feelings

Sour flower as sore eros rose.

Proper Names

Abba and Baboo

Displayed at the Entrance to the Pavilion of Abject Objects

A Cemetery Guardhouse

Lovers

More, more, mi amore, and never ever stop to keep score.

Dime Store Romance

She paid and stayed, while he played and played.

Concert

Rapped, wrapped, rapt

Dilemma

Do you swear to tell the whole truth filled with nothing but lies?

Haiku (1)

Clomp, clomp, stump, clump, knock
Fiddle meddle in muddle
slam, clump, stump, stomp, stomp

Haiku (2)

Red, yellow, and blue
Orange, eggplant, Granny Smith
Vermillion chartreuse

Biography

After X became Y, the name was entered into a registry, which was lost
in the San Francisco Earthquake.

Do Me a Favor

Change the color of your thoughts before they become inflamed,
and you volunteer to clomp south toward the fiery polar cap.

Beside the Remains of a Pumice Tower

Scarlet moss, but never a flower

A Fleet of Droll Skeletons Out for a Stroll

Our intelligence still marinating in a wooden bowl

Rodents begin to look quite incredible

when they are no longer edible.

I must decline your offer of leeks and lemur

I don't eat food cooked in an aluminum steamer.

Heaven's Carcass Flung Down from the Temple

How shall I write up this latest example?

Question

Who's going next said no one in particular to someone special.

Question (2)

Is she approaching or melting away?

Question (3)

Is this not the place where each of them is not seeing any other self instead of you and I?

Question (4)

Is being two things the same as believing you are feeling something inside?

Riddle

What do you ask of a frog that sticks its tongue out at you?

Announcement

Someone with the same name will give my lecture.

Graffiti Blues

O Bliss, why are you smiling
when it's you I'll soon be defiling?

The Other Shoe

You can't decide how to practice waiting for this.

Don't Have a Fit

when real love doesn't fit you like a glove.

Company Motto

This year's bonus
is next year's onus

Unspeakable Gifts

She did not anticipate that her anticipation would take such a drastic and monstrous form.

O My Little Worry Bead

Where will all my counting take me, if not that much closer to infinity?

Portrait

They were just doing this thing called kissing.

Once You Hang Your Trash Out to Dry

Can you turn around, go home, and forget how to sigh?

Mr. Flummox Begins His Lecture

In this poem, I do not rhyme "chance" and "dance," nor do I use the words "last, lest, or lust."

Jailhouse Fairy Tale

Once upon a time, a broken-down drunk met a skunk in a real stinker.

Chorus

I didn't know that I didn't know.

Familiar Family Fare

They were telling her what she was feeling, but she wasn't there.

Fairy Tale

The oldest elf wasn't getting any older any longer.

Exclusive

I would like to inform you that my client expects some other pronouns to become available at your earliest convenience.

Vermillion

It is sometimes necessary to adjust the mixture of dragon's blood and elephant's blood when they are fighting each other.

Foundation

Flake white, shell white, silver white, Venetian white

I Was Born in Hell's Kitchen

And I never did leave.

Testimony

He did all that, but that was not all that he did.

Old Man

My white hair touches the moon, but no one notices.

Old Woman

I can't stomach the sounds of spring.

Guest of Honor

Monsieur Crocodile grins and grins
While his frightened host begins
Detailing his many, many sins.

Marginalia

Escapade, Escalate, Escalator

My Name Is Icarus

I once flew too close to you to learn your name.

The World Is Our Oyster

rotting in the sun.

Exhibits

There is a good reason why a "Table of Contents" isn't included in tonight's menu.

.

Internet access is free as long as you answer a few simple questions.

.

Are you tired of being a conduit for a nameless god?

.

When was the last time you revealed your desire to be an intermediate creature dwelling between rock and slime?

.

When are you going to stop yelling "fire" in the middle of a crowded idea?

.

If you are reading this sign, you must stand and wait your turn.

.

Our fully licensed and legal union can reunite you with nearly all your lost opportunities.

.

There is nothing simpler and more human than an indecipherable theorem.

.

This is an opportunity to try not recognizing yourself in the mirror.

.

The unthinkable is a good place to start.

.

How about one for one, and all for nothing?

.

Do you think setting your trash on fire might be the best response
to spontaneous combustion?

.

Have you ever felt like a bucket of water at a fire sale?

.

We can still remove the gleam in your eye at no extra cost.

.

It is good to remember that tears of confusion are often uninvited guests.

.

In between these outbursts is someone else, but he's indistinguishable in
the dark.

.

The only place to have a nosebleed is in heaven.

.

Barking up the wrong tree is an inexpensive way to achieve a gratifying sexual climax.

.

Shall we begin the latest installment of this debate by exchanging branches of literature?

.

Swarms of thoughts came and left, and once in a while I managed to join them.

.

My specialty is factual smugness mixed with the latest news.

.

They will eat anything, even their neighbor's guinea pig.

.

Sculpture is a different story.

.

I wasn't always a carpet in a maze of darkness.

.

Although they remain chronically popular, mournful violins are no longer able to achieve the desired effect.

.

I do not follow hearses.

.

A small mule with an affable smile was the first to seduce me.

.

Would you like another onion ring or is this the last straw?

.

If you look through a microscope, you will see that I am more than just a donut covered in rainbow sprinkles.

.

Eventually, a large football-shaped device disguised as an eye will scrutinize everybody.

.

They were scared to death, and their pleasant demeanor certainly didn't help them.

.

According to the Inventory Data we have on hand, you are not yet born.

.

A smile is worming its way into your face.

.

I don't know exactly when I began talking to shadows
or stopped following myself into the bathroom to meet my destiny.

.

I am counting on these episodes to fulfill me.

.

Being called a "dirtball" is the least of your worries.

.

Please pardon my reappearance.

.

At least I haven't sprung any noticeable leaks.

.

Don't become part of the baggage you haul around.

.

You should always pack enough supplies in case you run out.

.

Can you give us a meter reading that ensures a comfortable future?

.

The unthinkable is approaching.

.

Leave a message when you've reached the end of your rope.

.

Being nude at all times of the day and night is a big responsibility.

.

If you are not in perfect shape, there's still a lot to be desired.

.

Don't abandon me for a plate of seaweed salad and golden fish sticks.

.

We regret to inform you that you are no longer in stock.

.

There is more to me than flees the eye.

.

Your idea of relief is a hideous joke.

.

Don't button your shirt when you are trying to start a conversation
with a stranger.

.

Don't hand over the cash until I say "Gimme all you got."

.

Bad breath is just a small part of why people scream at the sight of you.

.

Is that a curlew dangling from your talons?

.

You should begin the day with burnt toast because the carbon
helps you digest foreign substances.

.

Isn't it time we begin considering alternative sources of synergy?

.

If the highway rises up to meet you, you have probably taken the wrong exit.

.

When the carrot and stick method fails, try axle grease.

.

When all else fails, remove subject until your inquiry is answered.

.

Surgical precision can help find what you are looking for without consulting a phonebook.

.

Internal combustion led to the invention of digressive advances.

.

If that's music to your ears, then you need another handkerchief.

.

Can you name which country uses selective amnesia to determine its foreign policy?

.

Money has become a vast dirty sea rolling over the land.

.

Money has become a UFO because it is the only thing that lacks controversy.

.

Money rhymes with algae.

.

Do you swear to tell the whole truth filled with nothing but reasonable lies?

.

Signing up for Free Membership works best in a failing economy.

.

In case of emergency, please vacuum the premises.

.

I used to be thorough, now I am just comprehensive.

.

It's one thing to be blown off the face of the earth and another to have your face erased.

.

Who wants to complain when the sun ascends the ladder to the roadside drop-off where people sacrifice their life savings for an extra day at the beach?

.

It's supposed to add up, but not in the way you think.

.

Why make a spectacle of yourself when lightning strikes us all?

.

The conventioneers dispersed, their small feet carrying them to their assigned rooms.

.

At the Summer Palace we saw a pile of heads that looked familiar.

.

The pyramids are another example of forward thinking.

.

Do not overestimate your chatter now that there's dust on your hands.

.

Don't be the latest shovel of wet cement to remove itself from the picture.

.

Don't open any windows unless you mean it.

.

Don't be a sap unless you are planning on turning into syrup.

.

Being a guest is no excuse for acting like a salvageable resource.

.

My job is to prevent you from accessing your tension.

.

Is today's lesson plan any less of a plan?

.

At last the awful sunshine has been removed from the plastic flowers.

.

So begins a recent corruption.

.

Shall we twirl up some spaghetti and fling it over the wall,
hope that it lands on the heads of them all?

.

Trip wires (protruding legs) and land mines (the aforementioned
heads) line the odyssey to the bathroom.

.

Try and be patient when courtesy leaves you for another relapse.

.

Privilege is a form of indecision disguised as a necessity.

.

Smudges are the latest sign of sanctioned inactivity.

.

Don't let me catch you weeping on the job.

.

Employees must ash their hands before returning to the barracks.

.

Guillotine operators are encouraged to place their comments
in the proper suggestion box.

.

Butterflies continue feeding on the corpses of old statues.

.

Please accept this bowl of pink mucilage as a small token of my respect.

.

Have you ever considered the possibility that an alien life force might
welcome you?

.

I believe there is a secret relationship between pronouns.

.

Now that you mention it, I hate plums, especially when they are round
and sweet.

.

Two roads suspended operations in a yellow wood.

.

I did not think for us all.

.

I don't know who repeated these stories.

·

Kisses derangement farewell

·

There will be no more "Coming Attractions" until further notice.

·

Did you smile when the last token of affection dropped from heaven's empty vault?

·

Should eyes even be telling you this?

·

Soon you will be older than you were yesterday.

·

Do me a favor, and change the color of your thoughts before they become inflamed.

·

Starting tomorrow, individuals will be cancelled at an alarming rate.

·

Inscriptions drip down from the trees.

The Book of the Anonymous

1.

No way is the only way only a way
There is no way no name to its here
Which is everywhere we are not

2.

Light and dark are names there are
No names, divisions, harmonies
That embrace each instance of here

3.

Saying that one should or should not
Saying this prevents that
Saying no to everything including this

4.

Emptiness is a picture of something
That can be named, merged with something
That cannot be named

5.

Heaven and earth are names of places
Ways of dividing everywhere into here and there
There is no here there

6.

Naming the spirit is not the way
Unless the name is a thing
That cannot be named

7.

Do the names heaven and earth last forever
Or do they last as long as they are
Useful, misused

8.

All our names
Are written
On water

9.

Accumulation encloses one
In an emptiness
Merged with things that can be named

10.

Soul is a name, a wish
No wishes, no names
Is only a way

11.

Numbers become ways of looking
For names hidden in the vase
Which is empty

12.

To let go, to hold that, to choose, to push away
These are divisions and harmonies
The emptying of names

13.

Misfortune comes from having a body
Fortunate enough to dwell
In the pleasure of the nameless

14.

The image that is tangible and invisible
Is this also a way of naming
Can names be left behind

15.

Appearances can be named
We all make appearances
What other deceptions do we bring

16.

Do we become our names
Black swirls writhing on a white page
When our names are written on water

17.

We did not name
What we did
We did not have to

18.

Loyalty and disloyalty are necessary names
When there is no way, only directions
To the wished-for there

19.

Isn't water just a name
For the formlessness
We become

20.

What is this I
Aimless as water
Nourishing itself

21.

Where to begin
Forgetting the names
That cannot be forgotten

22.

All things will come to you
When they are not things
And you are not you

23.

Heaven and earth
Do not make things eternal
They are names of wishes

24.

Humans crawl on earth
Earth floats in sky
Sky is one name for the nameless

PART FOUR
The Missing Portrait

The Missing Portrait (1)

It does not do you like it
Imperfect copy's forgery
Posts its vermillion decree
These anointed mistakes
Neither robust nor enticing
These dark orthogonals and parallel curves
This swift recession to the single
Disgusted, the poem closes its mouth
Full of revulsion, the poem proceeds to close its eyes and ears
Once it recognizes, it realizes
Escape is impossible
Snow continues falling inside the glass egg
The villagers are singing, but the children looking in cannot hear them
Someone calls this poetry
Someone said, you shall observe words
Stealing parts of language that remain missing
Why speak about the unspeakable and the silence surrounding it
The unspeakable is a planet, our destination,
And silence is its atmosphere
The poem's mouth remains closed
There is no map that the poem can follow
The poem is a dog that doesn't sniff the traces of fear clinging to us
A man decides to paint a tree while the radio announces the progress of a war
A critic writes *you do not make progress painting a tree*
A new machine is progress, a machine of words
Each more perfectly realized than the last, is progress
Another example might begin with
I returned the tree to the hill from which it was stolen
Stay, coward blood, and do not yield to beauty's burning field
(I did not write this and neither did you)
And this latest example to arrive
The end is never near because it has always

Now the sky drifts out of the picture
Now the poem mangles its imperfect copy

The Missing Portrait (2)

It is not I nor the cloak in which this is wrapped
Now the sky drifts out of the picture
A window is all that remains
As much as could there was until now
The painting invites you
To refuse its refutation
Bond between inside now outside
It is often however very likely not
Now the window is closed and papered over
Arsenic orange is the ravenous fire of color
A spiral of birds rises from a dead man's perfect mouth
Who is omitted and who is permitted are other stories
Not told not old
Includes today and tomorrow
Not yesterday, at least as far as can be remembered
The tree cannot be painted
Verdigris, mars black, rose madder
Who shows us the skin breathing
Who shows us the room in which we are standing
Looking at what is before us, a painting
In which there is a room in which we are standing
I was not permitted or I *is* not permitted
If not the I, whose permission is being sought
Orpheus lost Eurydice because he did not turn back
Quartz, gypsum, calcite crystals
A porcelain vase made of fine grains
Suspended in an aqueous yellow binder
The name for this color went out of use
Around the time before clouds
Erased sky from its vocabulary
What is the name of the song you refuse to remember
Have forgotten nobody was blamed
And who or what is it that opens, flowerlike, in the land of words

Where does one go to contemplate a reflection of a reflection
This mirror held up to the sky, and the sky offering its mirror
He dreamed he was becoming a word written in a book
Burning pages rushed to greet him
It is raining outlined in cadmium red

The Missing Portrait (3)

The impermissible
Stares back at itself
From the mirror
It is not in
To obtain
This dimension
I had to transport a world
Its rivers and trees
Into its opposite
Opportunity distress exile
Where I observed birds
Spell the likeness of things
Backward into fire
Without consuming
Human shadow
I know just how their wishes
Will not come with any answer
Not known whether on panel
Parchment, canvas, or paper
Nor what medium
Nor what happened
Thought to be an identical copy
Of one that garnered treatises
Each letter a grain of wheat
Often torn in two
A room to which the eye has no access
Small brush suspended
From chandelier's gleam
Not in it only a reflection leaving
Jeweled blue paint
Changes place
In the center of
Not in the center of

This too is lost
Who will decline beguile additional disturbance
The world paints itself upon introduction
Wings are veins studded with eyes
Their words embroidered in clouds
Flecked with sunlight
Almost all of which did not allow names to come forth
Volcanic ejecta, pyrite, tiny prisms
Succumbing to fungi
Polished chalk skin
What can they do when our need is blessing
The sky reflected in the mirror
Is painted the color of the mirror's eye

The Missing Portrait (4)

Air of living dread
But if they yes they will
I should not again why
Rumored to be on wood
With doors that close
Glossy misnomers circulate
The entire world
Flattened and mapped
Concentric paint
Helpless against insects
Had the painting
Rustling red toxin
Endured dull fury
For an authentic effigy
To witness their reflection
Damaged parapet
Enclosed with no amount
Countenance words constantly
Changing their meaning
In the middle of now between
Seven steps lead to cellblock
Pluvial meadow's enamel sheen
Only a few are walking
Down a hill toward a town
That will never rise before them

I have been a house
A culvert in the foreground
Dotted vestiges of a sphere
That passed across proscenium night
Nowhere did I describe emotions

The Missing Portrait (5)

Only in curved world
Can tiny pearls (tears)
Float in green-tiled air
Their orthochromatic splendors
Housed in turning page
When centers of their circles
Lie outside their circumferences
Orpiment toads with heart-shaped tongues
Foam found only when moon is waning
Pressure from graduating reds
The horizontal stream winding through
Recently devastated suburbs of paradise
Does not reflect rainbow
Rivulets melting above second horizon
Incised within painted scene
Uncertain relationship between
Geological layers
Mouse gray and soot black
Penetrated by light
Coming from within
Mirror's rounded cheek
Bird's-eye view banishes
Shadows into background
Its separate compartments
Echo inside window
Neither open nor closed

PART FIVE
Further Adventures in Monochrome

Further Adventures in Monochrome

1)

My fundamental self is at war with my multiple personalities
I love everything that does not belong to me, which is to say my life

but I despise everything that belongs to me:
education, inherited psychology, physical attributes

In short, anything that is me because of exterior circumstances
My multiple selves are at war with my fundamental personality

because one is never only one. I am aware that in writing this
I have committed an error of diplomacy

I recognize that people will claim these notes and thoughts are confused,
poorly expressed (as if expression has anything to do with it), emphatic,

for they have been written day by day,
even during the rain that threatens to close down the sky

I know that many will regard these statements
as another example of bad taste

a poor substitute for poetry
when in fact poetry is not what I am after

My fundamental self despises all that belongs to me:
multiple personalities, butterflies, and silent hoarding

each more poorly expressed than the previous error of diplomacy
who claims these notes are inherited circumstances

My multiple selves are at war with substitutes for poetry
My fundamental self is at war with poems offered as substitutes

I know that many will conclude these statements do not belong to me
I am aware in writing this during the rain that it is not raining

2)

At present my paintings are invisible.
I do not speak
In a utopian manner
In proposing such a program.
My paintings remain invisible;
And I wish to display them
In a clear and positive manner.
Everything I write today
Precedes this presentation.
My propositions are landscapes of freedom.
I will say it again.
I want to show man in nature
With the traces and marks
He leaves behind,
Traces and marks
That are always marvelous, artificial,
Ephemeral, and yet indestructible.
Perhaps it seems to you
That I am attempting
The impossible,
That I am throwing myself
Toward something that is inhuman.
I had no affection for oil paint.
The colors seemed dead to me.
Yet art is the glue that holds
The entire universe together.
At present my paintings are invisible,
Which is why I decided
To penetrate still further
Into this landscape.
The physical painting
Gives its right to exist to one single fact,
That one believes only

In the visible,
While quite obscurely
Sensing the essential
Presence of something else,
At times almost invisible.
The painter is the one who knows
How to speak of that real value.

3)

I recently
declared
that the
artist of tomorrow
will continuously
re-create herself
by being able
to levitate.
I have already
made the first steps
toward work of this type.
I commanded
my living brushes
by remote control.

4)

I dwell in possibility, Emily Dickinson

I dwell in impossibility, Yves Klein

You should understand that I did not want you to read a painting. I wanted you to bathe in it before words domesticated the experience, and you turned to such stand-bys as "illumination" and "transcendent" to describe what happened to you. Painting should not be sentenced to sentences.

Painting is COLOR, I yelled at my first champion and biggest supporter. COLOR banishes words from its domain. When you read a painting, you turn it into language, but there is so much that cannot be turned into language that each of us experiences every day.

Red shadows leak out of rusting cars and collapsed bridges.
Green smoke rises from behind horizons and rooftops.
The spectrum of your mother's voice the last time she spoke to you.

Every day there are thresholds that you must cross to reach the domain where words mar every transmission, rendering them intangible.
We put our memory of these reverberations aside in favor of what is known and, we believe, knowable. We say we are going to the beach and we will look at the ocean and leave indentations in the sand, but that is not what happens. We go there to ponder a blue parcel cut from infinity.

True poets and artists know where language ends, which is why they go there. Some settle for going beyond the possible into possibility, but others want to dwell in the impossible. I am not talking fantasy here, because that version of the impossible is just a story about a girl named Thumbelina or a boy named Jack. The ones who go to where two roads diverge in a yellow wood are not poets, because they believe that experience can be reduced to a lesson about choices. True poets know that language is neither window nor mirror. The mistake is to believe that the opposite is true, that words (or signs) are arbitrary.

———————————————

This is my example of why words are not arbitrary. Charles Baudelaire believed that there are perfumes for which all matter is porous. These perfumes can permeate the air of one's dreams. Our thoughts quiver in the shadows that fall over us; they begin to free their wings and rise in flight, tinged with azure, glazed with rose, spangled with gold.

Azure, Rose, Gold.

I was not thinking of Baudelaire when I made my paintings, but the poet was clearly dreaming of me when he sat at his desk and wrote "The Perfume Flask."

Can't you see that this is how I, radiating outward, happened to appear on this planet, this speck of dust? Yves Klein was born because Baudelaire predicted this propitious event by naming colors, which, like all colors, escape the confines of their names, becoming more than an emanation of infinity. Even black can get away from its name, which is why Malevich had to surround it with white. But what is color that isn't surrounded by another color? What is that boundless world we catch a glimpse of whenever we look up at the sky? Is it so vast that we must turn away from it, afraid that it will swallow us up, which it will? Astronomy, the Greeks believed, was a royal science, which means I am a royal painter. Do not confuse me, however, with a painter of royalty, with Ingres, who used lines to hold and improve the faces of his sitters, who believed in the despotic power of beauty.

I am not interested in beauty. I am not Andy Warhol. He longed for possibility, but was afraid of what it might tell him. I dwell in impossibility, and I want to be embraced by what it will tell me.

My name is Yves Klein. There is a photograph of me that you might know. I have put on my best suit and jumped out a window. My arms are outspread, but they are not wings. I don't need them to fly. Nor am I the prince of clouds, Baudelaire's albatross, fallen from the sky. Screw that fascist Marinetti. My arms are not the wings of a drunkard beating against the wall. Mine are the outstretched arms of a diver. I fall effortlessly through the air, but I never am completely fallen. The cobblestones and I will never meet. I hover in a miracle, which is why you believe in the photograph, even after you have learned how I tricked you. It wasn't that hard to do. The true magician shows everyone how the trick was done, and after seeing how you were deceived, you believe in the trick all the more. I jumped out the window and I stayed in the air, which is where you wanted me to stay. I dwell in impossibility—that zone that lies beyond here and there, while embracing both.

5)

Everything exists to end up in a book, Stephane Mallarme

Nothing exists except in a book, which is the imagination, Yves Klein

In 1954, with the help of my aunt, I published two books, *Yves Peintures* and *Haguenault Peintures*. They documented the paintings I wanted to preserve in the impossible, the only domain we should long for. The preface for each book was made of thick black lines, rather than words, which links the books to Mallarme: *An insinuation simple   in the silence.* The purported author of the prefaces was Claude Pascal (or Pascal Claude). His name links him to the philosopher who wrote: "Contradiction is not a sign of falsity, nor the lack of contradiction a sign of truth." It is said that you can't have it both ways, but they are wrong. The infinite sky shows us this with every sun shower.

Each book has ten tipped-in color plates. In *Yves Peintures*, each plate is signed "Yves" and the name of a city in the lower right-hand corner. It might be where I made these paintings of colored paper. Isn't that what happens to a painting when it is put in a book? It becomes a piece of colored paper. So why not show that?

Each tipped-in plate is a piece of colored paper pointing to a monochromatic painting that never existed, except in the mind's eye. (Isn't this the only eye with which one sees?)

To make love is to be neither abstract nor literal.

To argue over whether the paintings existed or not is to miss the point. It is like arguing over how many angels can dance on the head of a pin when everyone knows that infinity is not a number, but a feeling, at once overwhelming and elusive, impossible to grasp and equally

impossible to avoid. Just try sitting alone in a bath for an hour with no
one in the next room.

Walt Whitman embraced multitudes and sang the body electric. But to
embrace infinity knowing that it will embrace you (and that it begins
to do so long before you arrived in this quadrant) is the song I want
to sing—its single note followed by a silence of equal length, a silence
that, as John Cage whispered, can never be silent.

That the paintings did not exist should have sent you
on the road to the impossible.
Where would you turn if you could not see them?
I wanted you to see what could not be seen,
to glimpse that fact, to be touched by something small and vast,
and know that you are somewhere between them,
moving in both directions at the same time.

6)

For beauty is nothing but
The beginning of terror, that we are still able to bear,
And we revere it so, because it calmly disdains
To destroy us.

Rainer Maria Rilke

I embrace the sky, which sees and seizes the blue inside my head.

Yves Klein

This is what I wrote in 1954, before Pollock died and Warhol ascended to the throne and became a household name: "I want to believe that in the future one will get to painting only paintings of one color at a time and without anything other than color... In literature there might be a way to get to the same point...a funny novel without plot, without closure, without subject, without message, and only with an atmosphere, a feeling of the same quality, very regular, profound and unified."

After reading this statement, why would anyone think that I believed that painting was dead or that I wanted to kill it?

If painting actually died, it would be the subject of a poorly conceived novel with a bulky plot.

There would be a convoluted roll call of antagonists and protagonists. There would be eyewitnesses, each of them eager to testify as to the veracity of the reports. Everything in this book would be predictable, from the color of the sky to predicting what would happen after the inevitable death of painting.

Other books would focus on painting's last days and hours, and report on those who were crowded at its deathbed. Detailed descriptions of gleeful outbursts would be properly annotated. Someone would claim that he or she was there, dressed for the occasion. Further reports and detailed footnotes would be added.

Who among us will cry out that it is easier to live in a world where painting is dead, and pretend to lament its loss?

7)

Yves Klein Blue (Interlude)

Bevel slue inky

Been veil sulky

Bye venue skill

Bilk evenly use

Bulk eye snivel

Buys eleven ilk

Blues like envy

8)

For me colors are living beings,
highly evolved individuals

that integrate themselves
with us, as with everything

What is a painting cut up
into small, monochromatic sections,

which are then used as pieces
in a jigsaw puzzle?

What is a monochromatic painting
cut up into small pieces,

which are then used
to reassemble the sky?

What is a tribe of people
who see one color at a time?

What becomes of a nebula
mistaken for a dangling curl of hair?

Why is a name given
to the stuff of which the sky is made?

What does it mean to say
"blue is akin to the sky"?

What is virtuous, moral, and chaste
in a sedentary manner?

Your verses begin
answering the chiming sky

Ill-formed words
gather around the black bile

9)

The blue we bathe in is the blue we breathe. The blue we breathe, I fear, is what we want from life and find only in fiction. For the voyeur, fiction is what's called going all the way.

William Gass

Blue is not a color, but the acceptance that one is dissolving into the infinite. This is why I am blue and breathing.

Yves Klein

A few months ago, for example, I felt the urge to register the signs of atmospheric behavior by recording on canvas the instantaneous traces of spring showers, of south winds, and lightning. (Needless to say, the last-mentioned ended in a catastrophe.) For instance, a trip from Paris to Nice might have been a waste of time had I not spent it profitably recording the wind. I placed a canvas, freshly coated with paint, upon the roof of my white Citroen. As I zoomed down Route National 7 at the speed of 100 kilometers an hour, the heat, the cold, the light, the wind, and the rain all combined to age my canvas prematurely. At least thirty to forty years were condensed into one day. The only thing annoying about this project is that I have to travel with my painting all the time.

The problem with traveling with a painting on the roof of your car all the time is that you cannot get out of your car until the paint is dry. A car, in fact, is a rather poor vehicle to carry you to infinity, because you might lose your way, like James Dean or Jackson Pollock, or you might have to stop for gas, its black smoke. I am not like Dean or Pollock. I want to be embraced by infinity, not run into it. That is because I dream of passing through its final barrier, like Baudelaire's perfume, and emerging on the other side.

To reach this place you must send your thoughts toward the sky. You must believe that no bird will cross their path as your thoughts ascend, higher and higher, shedding their colors as they climb toward home.

10)

(Robert Desnos and Yves Klein meet in the sky)

This beautiful summer afternoon is merely a witness
that records what occurs

The sky a silent and static state impressed by the very essence of movement

A tidal wave of color represented by the frenzy of the useless

A tidal wave, which all artists employ, is a sensory surface

Artists, in their chemical state, are mediums that the sky witnesses

The flame of poetry is washing the houses, sea, and clouds

11)

Trakl, Desnos, Klein

I was not a rosy little child who liked burying the sun
in the forest behind cobblestones and horseshoes

At twenty, I did not set up my easel at the bend in the road,
near the rotting huts

At thirty, I did not stop and photograph a green sun
sinking behind a blue snowdrift knocking at the door of immersion

My initiation began with clouds hovering in a blue garden
at the end of the world

Pale blue scents drifted into the sound of pumps punctuating the night

Blue shadows bloomed on the windowsill overlooking the funeral pyres,
their dancing blossoms

A little blue lamp shined its piece of bread on a child pleading with sentries

I believe Orpheus had just brushed the lute with his blue lips
when a door opened behind me

Inside, blue was infinity becoming silent and visible
among the rows of chattering trees

The blue of the sky, if we were to examine its many image values, would require a long study in which we would see all the types of material imagination being determined according to the basic elements of water, fire, earth, air. Basic elements of imagination. Blue study. Basic material. The study of and in. According to the blue of the material imagination. In which the air types its image: Imagination would require imagination to study all elements basic to the sky. A long study determined by water, fire, earth, air. Image values sky. In which would be determined material blue. Of blue fire in blue earth. Of blue earth in water and air. According to the sky, we would study all the types of elements basic to the imagination. According to the blue fire, we would see the material imagination in the sky. Its many image values. A sky in which we would see the imagination, the basic blue air. The image values its study of fire. All types of elements in the sky. If we were to examine the imagination we would see fire in air and water. Types of earth. Many values require basic study. According to the study in which we see all types of images. We according to the basic elements of we. Blue imagination. Fire requires earth. With water on air. Imagination requires we see air of sky. Sky on which the sky types: blue material imagination.

13)

An alchemist understands why I wrote: "My paintings are the 'ashes' of my 'art.'" Fire, earth, air, water circulate among each other. Fire is necessary for the transmutation of matter into spirit or what the materialists focus on: turning lead into gold. The materialists never admit to reversing the process, and turning gold into lead. I am being polite. I am not a materialist. I turned my paintings into "ashes" in order to rise through the sky toward the blue that waited on the other side of what I could see. An alchemist dwells in the possible, while I inhabit the impossible, intoxicated on color. That is why I am not an alchemist. I was born in an atomic age where all matter can suddenly vanish to leave behind nothing but what can be imagined. I want to live inside the serene color that emerges after the sudden flash of light that spreads across this planet, turning it to ashes. The painting's blue world.

14)

What I wanted from art was impossible. It is what every artist wants. If you settle for the possible, then your failure is ordinary, although, in a few cases, spectacular. I didn't want what was there for the taking, the images of things that could be named. I didn't want to add names to the vocabulary.

I rejected the ordinary and the extraordinary, because those are rungs one learns how to climb. I do not need a ladder to reach the sky.

I rejected all of the tried and true ways because I wanted to attain a state that exceeded the dimensions by which we are bound to the earth. "Never anyone but you," the poet wrote, "despite stars and loneliness. Despite the trees mutilated at nightfall. Never anyone but you will follow her path, which is mine. The further you go the bigger your shadow gets." In a place where there are no shadows because there are no bodies, I wanted my shadow to embrace me; I wanted to dissolve in its cold, sweet embrace. I wanted to dwell in the everlasting impossible. This is why I am a realist, which is different from being a New Realist. I am not a New Realist, but a timeless one. Why? Because I believe in miracles. Therefore it should not come as a surprise that I do not consider myself an artist of the avant-garde. Anyone can be toilet trained. Look around you, and you will see that nearly everyone is toilet trained. Only artists who are toilet trained can have their work in a museum. Having work in a museum is not why I became an artist. I became an artist because I wanted what art couldn't give me: I wanted to be immersed in what I could not experience: the impossible.

15)

Cubism was not the logical extension of Cézanne.

My monochromes are not the logical extension of Malevich and Mondrian.

I am not the logical extension of Fred Klein and Marie Raymond,
despite the fact that they were my parents and they were painters.

Blue is not the logical extension of Piero della Francesca's vision of Mary's robe.

It is obscurity becoming visible.

I became visible when I chose to be invisible in (indivisible from) my paintings.

It was my ghost you saw, issuing instructions, standing behind a curtain,
wearing a suit, covering a nude woman in paint.

I was never visible, even now.

Infinity is not eternity, where you are suspended,
like a bridge between here and there.

Eternity is a place, but infinity is an event.

I wink at you from infinity.

John Yau is the author of twenty-four books of poetry, fiction, essays, and collaborations with visual artists. In 1999, he started Black Square Editions, a small press devoted to experimental writing, translations, and essays. He was the arts editor of the *Brooklyn Rail* (2007–2011), but left to help start the online magazine *Hyperallergic Weekend,* where he regularly posts his reviews and commentary. The National Endowment for the Arts, New York Foundation for the Arts, John Simon Guggenheim Memorial Foundation, Foundation for Contemporary Arts, and Creative Capital-Warhol Foundation have awarded him fellowships and grants for his poetry, fiction, and art criticism. He was named a Chevalier in the Order of Arts and Letters by France's Ministry of Culture in 2002. He teaches in the visual arts department of Mason Gross School of the Arts (Rutgers University). He and his family live in Manhattan.

Since 1972, Copper Canyon Press has fostered the work of emerging, established, and world-renowned poets for an expanding audience. The Press thrives with the generous patronage of readers, writers, booksellers, librarians, teachers, students, and funders — everyone who shares the belief that poetry is vital to language and living.

MAJOR SUPPORT HAS BEEN PROVIDED BY:

The Paul G. Allen Family Foundation

Amazon.com

Anonymous

Arcadia Fund

John Branch

Diana and Jay Broze

Beroz Ferrell & The Point, LLC

Mimi Gardner Gates

Carolyn and Robert Hedin

Golden Lasso, LLC

Gull Industries, Inc.
on behalf of William and Ruth True

Lannan Foundation

Rhoady and Jeanne Marie Lee

Maurer Family Foundation

National Endowment for the Arts

New Mexico Community Foundation

Penny and Jerry Peabody

Joseph C. Roberts

Cynthia Lovelace Sears and Frank Buxton

Washington State Arts Commission

Charles and Barbara Wright

To learn more about underwriting Copper Canyon Press titles,
please call 360-385-4925 ext. 103

The poems are set in Adobe Garamond Pro.
Book design and composition by Phil Kovacevich. Printed on
archival-quality paper at McNaughton & Gunn, Inc.

The Chinese character for poetry is made up of two parts:
"word" and "temple." It also serves as pressmark for
Copper Canyon Press.